Telekinesis for Beginners

Examples, Experiments, Instructions and Models

Contact: www.HarryEilenstein.de
Harry.Eilenstein@web.de
Harry Eilenstein at youtube

Production and publishing house: BoD – Books on Demand, Norderstedt

ISBN: 9783753491288

Table of Contents

1. Moving Objects without Touching Them

At least since the "Star Wars" movies, telekinesis is again a term for most people – or at least they have an image of it, even if they may not know this term.

The picture that is drawn in "Star Wars" of telekinesis is not quite correct – not that telekinesis is impossible, but it is subject to other principles.

1. a) The basic telekinesis experiment

In order to be able to talk meaningfully about telekinesis, i.e. about the "moving of objects by the will", one must have experienced it – only then one knows that what one is talking or reading or thinking about actually exists.

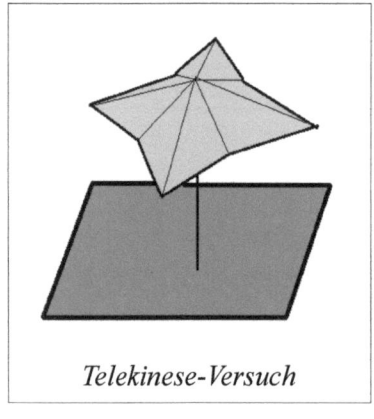

Telekinese-Versuch

Fortunately, there is a simple telekinesis exercise. For this experiment you need a piece of cardboard, a pin and a piece of paper that is 4cm·4cm in size.

Put the pin through the cardboard so that the pin is stuck vertically with the point upwards in the cardboard, which is lying on the table or on the floor. Bend the paper slightly in the two diagonals and in the two lines that divide the square piece of paper into two equal rectangles, so that the center of the piece of paper can be placed on the needle without falling off.

Then one holds a hand with short distance beside the paper wheel and turns then the wheel by telekinesis – videos to this attempt one can find with youtube under "telekinesis paper wheel" or "PSI wheel".

The actual telekinesis consists of wanting and imagining that the paper wheel is turning. However, this should not degenerate into strained or tense concentration. You can also do this experiment with several people – and if they laugh, it is even easier.

With some people the attempt works immediately, some need to watch a few videos about it beforehand, and still others need to have it demonstrated first by another person (like me).

This kind of thing is most easily learned by experiencing it, and by experiencing the "taste" of what's going on. This "taste" is impossible to convey through words – you can describe the taste of a ripe strawberry in detail, but someone who has never eaten a strawberry will still not know what it tastes like …

So: turn on the PC or tablet and take a look at the experiment. And then make a paper wheel and do the experiment yourself.

The paper wheel turns now, with which the telekinesis would be basically proved as a real phenomenon.

Now you can have a closer look at this experiment and see, what can be concluded from it and if there are further experiments resulting from these considerations.

1. b) Which resistances must telekinesis overcome?

Tekinesis must act in three ways to get the paper wheel to rotate:

1. Telekinesis must overcome the inertia of the resting paper wheel – the force of the telekinesis must accelerate the mass of the paper wheel. In principle, a constant force, if there are no other factors, should accelerate the wheel more and more, so that it becomes faster and faster. However, the paper wheel reaches its "standard speed" of about 1 revolution per second quite quickly and then stays at this speed.

The paper used for the paper wheel has a weight of approx. 80g/m2. The standard paper wheel with 4cm side length has therefore a weight, i.e. a mass of approximately 0.13g.

2. The effect of telekinesis is reduced by the friction of the paper on the tip of the needle. The friction factor between metal (needle tip) and paper is about 0.2, which means that about one fifth of the force of telekinesis is lost due to friction. Since this portion remains constant independent of the speed of the rotation, the rotation would have to accelerate the wheel more and more in spite of this friction – but it doesn't.

3. When the paper wheel rotates, there is also friction between the paper wheel and the air. In contrast to the friction between needle and paper, which always "swallows" about one fifth of the force, the air friction depends on the square of the rotation speed. Thus, air friction becomes four times as great at twice the speed, nine times as great at three times the speed, sixteen times as great at four times the speed, and so on.

The air friction leads to the fact that by a constant force, here the telekinesis, a rotation speed is reached, at which the "driving" by the telekinesis and the "braking" by the air resistance become equal. The result is a constant rotational speed.

1. c) Air friction

In order to check whether this third consideration is true in this form, one could carry out the paper wheel experiment at different air pressures, since the air friction also depends on the air density. Of course, the most interesting experiment would be a test in vacuum, because there the rotation of the wheel would have to increase. But also an experiment at 4000m altitude in the Alps would be informative, because the air pressure there has already dropped to 60% of the pressure at sea level.

So the rotation speed of the paper wheel up in the Alps should be much higher – if the theory that the air friction determines the rotation speed of the paper wheel is correct. (The rotation should be 1.3 times as fast as at sea level).

Unfortunately I have not been on a higher mountain for a long time and I have not found any other possibility like a room where you can regulate the air pressure.

Luckily my son David has had an idea how to do an experiment to measure the role the air friction plays in limiting the velocity of the rotation of the paper wheel:

> You can alter the paper wheel and add landing flaps to the sides of the wheel by folding over 1cm of the side of the wheel at an right angle. This enhances the air fraction considerably and should reduce the rotation of the wheel if the air friction plays a role in limiting the speed of rotation of the wheel.
> But the speed of rotation stays exactly the same.
> Conclusion: The constant speed of the rotation of the paper wheel of approximately one rotation per second is not caused by the air friction of the turning wheel.

1. d) The size of the paper wheel

In order to find rules, it is always helpful to vary a size in an experiment to see which change of the experimental result this will cause – in this way one can find quantitative correlations like "double the distance – only a quarter of the effect".

To find out which rules telekinesis follows in the paper wheel experiment, I cut papers with different side length: 1cm, 2cm, 3cm etc. up to 8cm. Then I looked at the rotation speed of these different paper wheels.

In the experiments that I have conducted so far together with about 50 people, the paper wheels with the standard side length of 4cm sidelength, which I have always used, have always achieved a rotation speed of just a little under 1 revolution per second.

In the series of tests with paper wheels of different sizes, it turned out that I can just about turn the 8cm wheel and that the two very small wheels cannot be moved at all. Of the six wheels I got to turn (3cm to 8cm), the smallest turned the fastest and the largest turned the slowest. Checking the turning speeds showed that a wheel with a side length twice as large and thus four times the size and mass of another wheel turned only a quarter as fast as the other.

The deviation of the measurements from the physical principle "double mass => half effect" was very accurate – the deviations were clearly below 5%.

This shows that also telekinesis behaves first of all like a normal physical force, whose effect depends linearly on the size of the mass to be moved.

1. e)   The posture of the hands

With myself and also with most of the other people with whom I have done this experiment so far, the paper wheel turns in the direction in which the fingers of the hand next to the wheel point. So if the right hand is to the right of the wheel, the wheel turns counterclockwise; if the left hand is to the left of the wheel, the wheel turns clockwise.

With a little skill, you can place your hands so that both palms face the wheel and the fingers both face counterclockwise or both face clockwise. In my experience, this is the most effective hand position.

It sounds as if life force is flowing through the palm from the base of the hand to the tips of the fingers, carrying the wheel along – like a kind of "life force watermill". This direction of flow of life force is also found, among other things, in the three acupucture meridians that run through the palm of the hand.

This explanation is nice, but it has a flaw: It is also possible to simply point a single finger in the direction in which the cog should turn – this can also work. One would think that a single finger would have only a fifth as much force as the whole hand, but this is not true – I have not noticed any significant difference in the speed of the wheel's rotation depending on the number of fingers used.

I have also seen some people place their left hand to the left of the wheel and their right hand to the right of the wheel, with the fingers of one hand pointing clockwise and the fingers of the other hand pointing counterclockwise. According to the life force flow theory, the telekinesis forces of the two hands should cancel each other out – but they don't always …

Sometimes the paper wheel is also "stubborn" and turns against the assumed direction of rotation – as if the life force in the hand would suddenly flow "the wrong way around".

1. f)   The distance of the hands

It is shown by performing experiments with different distances between the hands and the paper wheel that the speed of rotation is just as independent of the distance between the hands and the wheel as it is of the number of fingers stretched out next to the paper wheel.

However, from a distance of one to two hands lengths, the effect sometimes occurs that the paper wheel no longer wants to rotate. Up to this distance, however, it always rotates at approximately the same speed.

In physics, a force that spreads unbundled in all directions decreases quadratically with the distance: "double the distance => only a quarter of the effect".

So telekinesis does not behave like an unbundled physical force – like e.g. a magnetic field or like gravity. If telekinesis should follow the same rules as the physical forces, it would have to be a bundled force – like water in a tube, like electrons in a pipe or like the drawbar at a cart.

But the matter is even more complex: My son can even make the wheel turn by simply telling the wheel what to do and not putting his hand next to it at all (his physics teacher was rather speechless when he showed him this). This means that either my son can direct the life force only by his imagination or that the life force is perhaps even an inappropriate model to describe telekinesis.

Holding the hand next to the paper wheel is therefore possibly rather an imagination aid than a tool – a telekinesis ritual, so to speak, which one can also do without, but which is extremely practical and helpful for the beginner.

1. g)   The number of people

If one carries out the experiment with four people at the same time at one paper wheel, actually the fourfold force should act on the paper wheel, why it should turn four times as fast – no matter whether the telekinesis is a bundled or an unbundled force.

If one considers the dependence of the air friction on v^2 (square of the velocity), four people should still be able to make the cog turn about at least twice (instead of four times) as fast.

The wheel turns however completely independently of the number of persons always equally fast.

This shows that the whole matter is more complex than it might have seemed at first.

1. h) The number of paper wheels

The somewhat paradoxical situation from the previous experiment is confirmed by the fact that it is possible to have several paper wheels turning at the same time without slowing them down.

This can only be explained with the usual laws of nature from physics, if one assumes that telekinesis is not a directed force – just as a magnetic field can attract several iron particles at the same time, without this having an influence on the movements of the individual iron particles.

However, the experiment with varying the distance of the hands to the paper wheel has shown that telekinesis must be a concentrated force ("water pressure in a pipe"), because the effect of telekinesis is independent of the distance of the hands from the wheel.

So the experiment with the distance between the hands can only be explained by a bundled force ("water pressure in a pipe") and the experiment with different numbers of paper wheels or different numbers of hands only by an unbundled force ("magnetic field"). These two results contradict each other quite thoroughly …

From this it follows that telekinesis either follows completely different rules than those of physics, or that there is a superordinate model like the wave-particle-duality in physics, which resolves this contradiction.

In any case, this contradiction is extremely gratifying, since it contains two results for which a common description can now be sought – such a contradiction can open the gates to new insights in research.

1. i) The mass of the wheel

If you do this experiment with a paper wheel of 4cm·4cm but with a double sheet of paper, it rotates approximately half as fast as a wheel of 4cm·4cm whith only one sheet of paper. This was to be expected: "double the mass => half the rotation speed".

But if you cut this sheet into two paper wheels and put them on two needeles, they rotate wiht the "usual speed".

In an telekinesis experiment it seems to be important how large the single item is but not how many items there are.

1. j) The form of the wheel

The experiments with other forms of wheels have been a bit confusing:

If you cut a small and long wheel out of paper and put it on the top of the needle, it looks as if the rotation speed of the wheel does not depend on the size and thus on the mass of the wheel but on the the longest side of the wheel – the rotation speed of a 2cm·4cm-wheel sems to be the same as of a 4cm·4cm-wheel.

A small paper-strip of 1cm·20cm on a needle-point moved only a little bit. Also a paper-strip of 1cm·10cm rotated only a quarter of an circle.

It seems that the size of the paper wheels that can be easely rotated, is not only limited by the surface and thus the mass of the wheel, but also by the diameter of the wheel. Otherwise the 1cm·10cm-wheel should rotate approximately as fast as a 3cm·3cm-wheel.

This holds true also for a wheel in the form of a cross of 4cm·4cm with small sides that has half the mass compared to the normal wheel of 4cm·4cm. Both rotate with the same speed.

Does the rotation speed depend not on the mass of the wheel but on its size, that is on the diameter of the wheel?

At least there is one difference between the 4cm·4cm-wheel and the half as heavy 4cm·4cm-cross: The cross reaches distinctly sooner its final velocity.

1. k) Faraday cage

A Faraday cage is a box made of a metal wire mesh, which has the effect that it does not let electromagnetic forces pass through. However, placing the paper wheel in a Farday cage has no effect on spinning – which rules out the effect of an electromagnetic force.

1. l) Gravitation and strong nuclear force

These two forces can also be ruled out – gravitation because it is so weak and so uniform; and strong nuclear force (color force) because it does not act beyond the radius of an atomic nucleus.

The weak nuclear force can also be ruled out, because it is a different kind of force that changes things but does not attract things to each other.

1. m) The candle experiment

One could assume that the paper wheel is driven by the heat of the hands – like a Christmas pyramid. However, this is not the case for three reasons:

1. The speed of rotation does not depend on the distance of the hands from the paper wheel, which should be the case with a heat-actuated air flow.

2. Tea lights instead of hands cannot make the wheel turn.

3. In order to react to heat, the wheel would have to have the shape of a propeller – which is not the case.

1. n) Glass insulator

Placing the paper wheel under glass seems to effectively inhibit its turning – at least I have not seen anyone "live" (only on youtube) who has been able to turn a paper wheel under a glass. Glass thus seems to be a life force insulator …

Or is glass merely such a strong suggestion of isolation that telekinesis does not work?

1. o) Conclusions

Consequently, it seems that telekinesis on the receiving end reacts partly according to the normal physical rules:

- double mass => half speed

But telepathy seems to follw partly also its own rules:

- The rotation speed depends also on the form and diameter of the wheel.

On the transmitter side, however, telekinesis seems to be completely subject to other, non-physical rules:

- The hand posture, the number of fingers used and the hand proximity to the paper wheel are possibly only imagination aids – the turning speed is not dependent on them and it even works without the hands at all …

This questions the life force theory – or it presupposes that the life force does not have to be directed with the help of gestures. The posture of the hand and the gestures of the hands would then be a kind of "telekinesis ritual" – and it also works without ritual …

- The direction of rotation of the paper wheel is mostly in the direction of the fingers – but by no means always.

- Glass seems to be a telekinesis insulator – if the glass does not simply effectively suggest that it is life-force-impermeable …

- The independence of the turning speed from the distance of the hands speaks for a concentrated force ("water pressure in the pipe") – or just for the fact that the postures of the hand are only a "telekinesis ritual".

If one turns several paper wheels at the same time, these have the same speed as a single wheel. So the telekinesis must be an unbundled force ("magnetic field") – which contradicts the independence of the rotation speed of the paper wheel from the distance of the hands – except if the hand posture is only an imgination aid. This interpretation is also supported by the fact that it is also possible to simply tell the wheels what to do …

- The rotation speed of the paper wheel is not limited by the air friction.

Since four times as many people should also have four times as much telekinesis power as a single person, but the paper wheel always turns at the same speed, no matter who or how many turn the wheel, the air friction must

12

play a subordinate role.

Even landing flaps on the side of the wheel do not alter the rotational speed of the wheel and ruling thus out a greater role of the air friction in defining the constant speed of rotaion of a certain size of a paper wheel.

- The metal grid of a Faraday cage is not a telekinesis obstacle.

- There seems to be something like an "action constant" in telekinesis, which is:

> - independent of the number of moving objects,
> - independent of the number of people performing telekinesis,
> - independent of the number of hands or fingers used,
> - at least in principle also independent of the distance of the hands to the moved object, and
> - independent of the addition of landing flaps to the wheel and thus independent of the air friction.

On the receiver side telekinesis shows a "normal" behavior: double mass => half speed.

On the transmitter side, on the other hand, there is mainly a rotation speed constant, which seems to be independent of the posture and the distance of the hands, of the number of participating persons, of the number of wheels and of the addition of landing flaps to the wheel.

Whether the rotation speed is also dependent on the air pressure remains to be verified by experiments. Since four persons do not make the wheel turn twice or four times as fast, but just as fast as a single person, the air friction is very probably of a rather small importance.

It seems that at least the hand position and the distance of the hands to the paper wheel are only imagination aids for the "telekinesis ritual".

Possibly also glass is not a real life force insulator, but only the effective suggestion of such an insulator – however, this is by no means certain.

There are thus four results:

1. the "normal" dependence of the effect of telekinesis on the size of the moving mass (which is in accordance with the laws of physics),

2. the "un-normal" dependence of the effect of telekinesis on the form of the moving mass (which is rather probably not in accordance with the laws of physics),

3. the rotational velocity constant, which is very probably independent of the air friction,

4. the high probability that the gestures and the distance of the hands to the wheel are only imagination aids ("telekinesis ritual").

The most interesting point is the rotation speed constant, for whose existence no cause is recognizable at first.

2. The Telekinesis Constant

The most curious result of the previous considerations is the independence of the telekinetic effect from many factors, of which one would actually have to assume that they should have an influence:

- the number of persons involved,
- the number of paper wheels turned,
- the posture of the hands,
- the distance of the hands from the paper wheel,
- the air friction ("landing flaps"),
- the mass of the wheel – at least the form of the wheel (square, strip, cross) also has a large influence on the rotation velocity.

Above all, one should assume that the paper wheel rotates faster due to the added telekinesis force of several persons – but this is not the case.

One can now have a look what can be said about this constant.

First of all, this constant appears as a constant of rotation speed: The wheel of a certain size always turns at the same speed.

However, this constant is not absolute, but depends on the mass of the paper wheel. This means that this constant is on the side of the telekinesis sender and not on the side of the telekinesis receiver: The telekinetic force has a certain constant magnitude, whose visible effect depends on the mass of the moved object.

This telekinesis constant, surprisingly, seems to be the same for all people and even for all groups of people (e.g., four people turning one wheel).

Physical circumstances cannot be responsible for this constancy, since a larger acting force should also be seen to have a larger effect.

Thus, the telekinesis constant seems to exist independently of individual people and to be based on a property of the life force or something similar.

To better understand this constant, it might help if it could be related to other processes that are also constant.

Unfortunately, to my knowledge, there are no other telekinetic experiments known that could be studied in the same way as the paper wheel experiment. However, one can try to get further on with an indirect approach.

Telekinesis and telepathy react on will and imagination, i.e. they are connected with the psyche. Moreover, they are not exercised consciously, but unconsciously –

telepathy is a similar process as, for example, dream journeys or meditation: one connects the waking consciousness with the subconsciousness and then acts in the inner world, in which the dream images are also located.

This inner world of dream images, this inner archive of all memories, this inner space where all motivations are located, becomes visible in the EEG, i.e. in the measurement of (electrical) brain waves as a frequency of 4-8Hz with a mean value at 6Hz. Waking consciousness has 8-16Hz (mean: 12Hz), ecstasy as in panic, fighting or orgasm has 16-32Hz (mean: 24Hz) and deep sleep has 2-4Hz (mean: 3Hz). These four states of consciousness are octaves apart, so to speak – the frequency doubles from one kind of consciousness to the next:

deep sleep:	3Hz
dream state:	6Hz
waking:	12Hz
Ecstasy:	24Hz

The frequency of 6Hz appears in many places, all related to the "life (life force) of the body":

- dream state EEG
- laughter, crying, natural vibrato of the voice
- trembling, chattering teeth
- orgasm reflex
- trauma dissolution shaking
- epileptic seizures
- deep relaxation, astral projection

When one relaxes deeply and thus possibly also aims at astral projection, several phenomena occur one after the other:

1. The body becomes still.

2. The body becomes relaxed

3. The body becomes heavy.

4. The body becomes warm.

5. The body begins to vibrate at about 6Hz.

6. The body begins to twitch – but not the physical body, only the life force body (astral body). At the same time, the arms make impossible movements

such as briefly twitching down through the mattress and back up again – which clearly shows that although this feels like a physical movement, it is not a physical movement.

7. The body begins to sway back and forth or from side to side – again, this is only the life force body (astral body), as the bed continues to stand still.

8. The life-force body detaches from the physical body and one begins an astral projection.

-. The phenomena listed in point 1. to 4. are also used as suggestion in hypnosis.

This experiment shows that the 6Hz frequency is the natural vibration of the life force body – one can feel on's own astral body vibrate with the frequency of 6Hz.

This frequency, that also accures in laughter, weeping, chattering teeth and so on, is always about 6Hz – so it is a constant. However, the life force does not vibrate everywhere in the body with exactly this frequency – in the chakras other vibration frequencies or rotation frequencies can be experienced during meditation. However, the life force body as a whole always seems to vibrate with 6Hz.

Now the question arises, how the telekinesis constant could be connected with this frequency.

The simplest conceivable connection would be the oscillation formula from physics: "frequency · wavelength = speed". For example, if a wave oscillates 3 times per second and each of these waves is 10cm long, it travels 3·10cm in one second, i.e. the wave has a speed of 30cm/sec.

Since the telekinesis constant does not refer directly to the speed of rotation, but is a property of the acting force, i.e. the telekinesis, one can unfortunately not link the frequency of 6Hz and the speed of rotation of the paper wheel directly with each other. However, one can try to approach a connection of these two numbers.

First of all it is known that the acting telekinetic force is as large as the sum of the friction between needle and paper and the air friction.

The needle/paper friction also depends on the mass of the paper wheel, which is about 0.13g for a side length of 4cm.

The speed of rotation should actually depend on both the mass of the wheel (needle/paper friction) and presumably the air friction. However, the experiments so far seem to indicate that the speed of rotation depends only on the mass (and maybe on the diameter of the wheel) – the numbers in these experiments are so accurate that no influence of the higher air friction due to the larger paper wheel is visible.

The oscillation formula "frequency · wavelength = speed" also contains the quantity "wavelength". So it would be interesting to find a wavelength which is related to the vital force.

However, so far only one example is known to me for this, that is moreover somewhat uncertain. I myself and also an acquaintance of mine have observed several times during observations of the state of the chakras of other people that waves emanate from the chest space upwards and downwards. These waves start at the lower end of the sternum (wish tree – a minor chakra) and go up to the root chakra or start at the upper end of the sternum (thymus minor chakra) and go up to the crown chakra.

For a person sitting quietly this is about 20 waves, for a moving person about 35-40 waves.

Since both the distance chest – root chakra and the distance chest – crown chakra are approx. 40cm, this results in a wave length of 2cm (40cm : 20 waves = 2cm) for the resting state and a wave length of 1cm (40cm : 40 waves = 1cm) for the moving state.

Since these waves occur in connection with the chakras, they should be movements of the life force. Therefore, we can see what happens when we combine the 6Hz frequency of the life force with these wavelengths.

At 6Hz, i.e. at 6 waves per second, and a wavelength of 2cm, these waves move 6·2cm per second, i.e. they have a speed of 12cm/sec. With a wavelength of 1cm, on the other hand, the speed is 6cm/sec.

The constancy of the frequency means that the waves become slower when the wavelength becomes smaller.

In the resting state of the body, the flow velocity of the blood in the two main veins, which run from the chest upwards and downwards, respectively, is 12cm/sec, which corresponds exactly to the assumed expansion speed of the life force waves in the resting state. However, the flow velocity of the blood increases to 20cm/sec when the body is in motion – instead of decreasing to 6cm/sec … So there is no alignment here.

This finding is in contradiction to the behavior of waves in the physical field, because there the expansion speed of a wave and not the frequency of the wave is a constant – e.g. waves in the air propagate with the speed of sound of 1236km/h.

One can wonder at this point if all previous considerations have been correct (what is not at all sure):

- The independence of the rotation speed from the number of paper wheels and the number of persons is an experimental result and therefore certain.

- The 6Hz frequency, which has a maximum fluctuation of 4-8Hz, is well secured, because it appears at many places including the life force body.

- The wavelength of 2cm in the resting state or 1cm in the moving human being is not yet well secured, for it is only the inner perception of me and an acquaintance of mine. It would be desirable to secure this wavelength in a more solid way for example by physical phenomena.

On the basis of these considerations one can actually only say for sure that the telekinesis constant points to a still unknown regularity which works differently than the physical laws.

One can assume in addition with some certainty that the frequency of 6Hz has a great importance for the life force.

Finally, there is a third result: the object receiving the telekinetic force behaves according to the physical laws (double mass => half speed).

The change from the "telekinetic laws" with their curious constant to the physical laws is therefore between the telekinetic sender (human being) and the telekinetic receiver (moving object) – what is actually self-evident, but in this clarity nevertheless new.

The role that is played by the form and especially the diameter of the wheel, is unclear.

3. Multiplication of one's own Power

After the existence of telekinesis has been proved in principle by the paper wheel experiment, the influence of telekinesis in all extraordinary processes can now be used for explanation.

With the following considerations it is also interesting to pay attention whether additions to the five previous results can be concluded from them. These five results are:

     - the "mass dependence" of telekinesis
     - the "telekinesis constant"
     - the "life force frequency of 6Hz".
     - the "boundary between the telekinesis laws and the physics laws".
     - the "telekinesis ritual"

Ther is also the question:

     - What role play the form and diameter of the telekineticly moved object?

3. a) Smilie experiment

smilie

For this experiment you need two persons, a table, a sheet of paper and a pencil or similar.

With the pencil you draw the smilie shown on the left on a sheet of paper and then put the sheet on a table in such a way that you can see it clearly when you stand in front of the table.

One of the two persons stands in front of the table, stretches out both arms to the left and to the right ("cross posture") and looks at the smilie.

The second person stands behind the first person and places their hands on the first person's two elbows.

Then the second person pushes the arms of the first person down with all his strength. He will most likely not succeed.

upside down smilie

Now the smilie is turned 180°, i.e. upside down.

The attempt is now repeated – the person in the "cross posture" now has no chance of keeping his arms up …

These two attempts are then repeated with the roles reversed – the "pusher" is now in the "cross pose". By changing roles, both can see that there is a difference.

3. b) Shaolin experiment

For this experiment you need three persons and a table or similar.

One person puts his hand on the table – the other two people hold this hand on the table.

The held person tries with all his strength to pull his hand away from the table – but he has no chance against four hands that hold him.

Now the experiment is repeated in a slightly different way: The person being held turns away from the table (his hand is now more or less behind him) and stretches out his other arm in front of him so that he can look into the palm of his hand. While looking into his palm, he simply walks away from the table – the others cannot hold him …

3. c) "Hepp" experiment

In this experiment, one person lies down with his belly on the floor and a second person lies down with his belly on the heels and calves of the first person.

Now the first person tries to lift the second one up with their legs. I know of only one man who managed to do this – and got a severe pulled tendon … so you should not overdo this experiment, but consider your own constitution.

Then you make a second experiment in the same posture. As a preparation for this, the lying person imagines that a white ray of light is flowing from his or her parting of the hair to the soles of his or her feet and that there is only a small feather pillow on his or her legs. Then this first person inwardly says "Hepp!" (= Now! Jump! Go!) and lifts the second person up with his legs.

Since the legs are bent at the knees, it can happen that the second person gets so much momentum that he rolls up to the head of the lying person or beyond – so you should make sure that there is some space in front of the head of the lying person.

If someone is talented for the role of the "lying person", two or three "second persons" can also lay on top of each other on the first person's lower legs.

Like many other such experiments, the "hepp" experiment seems to succeed best when several people perform these attempts simultaneously in a larger group.

3. d) Jumps and the like

My son is a Parcour and Ninja warrior trainer, among other things, and bases his classes also on the "Hepp" experiment. If, for example, someone simply does not succeed in a certain jump, he advises the person concerned to sit down and imagine the desired jump as precisely, in detail, extensively and intensively as possible until the person concerned feels exactly how the jump he is striving for feels. Then, when this image has come alive in him, he stands up and makes this jump – just like that …
The inner image of the aspired and achieved goal directs the life force.

3. e) Karate

The "Hepp" principle is also used in Karate – this method is also an important element in the other Eastern martial arts, but in Karate it is especially visible and can be experienced.

Experiment 1: You take a stick and hit it on the ground to break it.
Then one repeats the experiment and imagines intensively beforehand that the stick breaks.

Experiment 2: One puts a stick between two walls, between two branch forks or similar and then hits the first stick with a second, stable stick or with a sword or similar to break it.
Then one repeats the attempt and imagines before intensively that the stick breaks.

Experiment 3: Now you try to break the stick not with a second stick, but with the edge of your hand.

Repeat the experiment and imagine that the stick is only a spider's thread and that you do not hit the stick or the spider's thread, but that you hit a point 20 cm below the stick (spider's thread) this is the imagination of the effortlessly reached goal.

In this attempt one should not exaggerate – the hand should remain intact …

It would seem that this experiment could be successfully performed even without any expertise:

> In my childhood, corporal punishment was still common. One evening, when I was about 5 years old and I was still telling stories and laughing in our beds with two of my sisters long after we were supposed to be asleep, my father came angrily into the room with his hazel stick and shouted, "Who wants a beating first?"
>
> For some reason unknown to me, I shouted at the top of my lungs, "Me! Me! Me!" and almost had a fit of laughter, to which my sisters then also responded with "Me! Me! Me!" and joined in.
>
> That made my father a bit uneasy, but he turned me onto my stomach anyway, pulled down my pajama pants and hit me with the cane – which, however, immediately broke into several pieces at the first blow, while I kept laughing the whole time.
>
> Then my father left silently – that was the end of caning in our family …

A few years later it happened to me again with an older woman whose kitchen spoon broke on my butt to pieces, although she didn't hit very hard.

3. f) Dice without chance

When playing "Ludo" with four of us, especially when my other children were present, sometimes a very special high-spirited mood arose, which was something like a "controlled laughing fit with clear direction". In this mood, wishes for certain numbers were constantly fulfilled – it sometimes happened that someone rolled ten "sixes" in a row.

After a while it became a bit more difficult, because whenever someone wished for a "two", for example, someone else imagined another point between the two "two"-points, so that it became a "three" … Only the "6" could not be "falsified" with this method.

The mood during these "dice games without coincidence" was quite similar to the mood during my laughing fit, when my father's cane broke.

3. g)   Levitation for beginners

This experiment is another variation of the "Hepp" experiment. In this experiment, one person sits down on a chair and puts his arms against his body and his hands on his thighs. Four other people put their hands together, make them into two fists, and then extend their two index fingers, which are next to each other. Then the four people put their "double index fingers" under the two armpits and the two knees of the first person and try to lift him up – which should hardly be possible …

Then the four persons put their hands one above the other on the head of the first person and concentrate for approximately half a minute – they can also sing an "a" together while doing this, but this is not absolutely necessary.
Then the four persons try again to lift the person om the chair – with a clearly different result …

3. h)   Lifting loads

You can also do this experiment with stones, beams and the like. I have heard of some successful attempts of this kind, but I have not yet performed this experiment myself.
Also this form of telekinesis seems to be possible without any previous knowledge. My father told me that once he saw a mother lifting a truck with one hand and with the other hand pulling her child out from under the tire of the truck, under which the child had gotten in an accident.

3. i)   The basic principle

The basic principle of all these experiments seems to be that one concentrates on the goal and not on the obstacle – that is, one aligns oneself with what one wants: will and imagination, that is, the image of the desired goal filled with the power of one's striving. In a sense, one inwardly creates the desired goal – one shapes the life force and thereby directs it.
There are several basic differences between the paper wheel experiment and the different variants of the "Hepp" experiment:

In the paper wheel experiment, a small effect is produced without the action of a physical force, whereas in the "Hepp" experiment, a physical effect is effortlessly magnified to a strength that is normally far beyond the realm of possibility.

The differences between these two experiments are in detail:

Differences of the Telekinesis Experiments		
Element	*Experiment*	
	Paper wheel experiment	*"Hepp" experiment*
Physical contact	no	yes
Acting force	telekinesis	body power and telekinesis
Effect	very small	very large
Accompanying phenomena	Concentration	concentration, laughter

3. j) Conclusions

What results from these experiments for the understanding of telekinesis?

- First of all, both telepathy and telekinesis are based on will and imagination.

- This orientation towards a goal can reach up to the unrestrained one-directedness of a laughing fit or the one-directedness of the motivation to save one's own child.

- Conducting the "Hepp" experiments in a group seems to increase the efficacy of these experiments. This is different to the paper wheel experiments, where four people do not turn the wheel any faster than one person.

The importance of this one-pointedness unity has also been succinctly stated by one of the most famous magic teachers – Master Yoda: *"Do or do not – there is no try."*

There is a curious phenomenon in the "Hepp" experiments which, to begin with, is anything but self-evident: Why is it that telekinesis can amplify a person's physical power many times over, when telekinesis is so decidedly weak without physical contact, as in the paper wheel experiments?

Does telekinesis need physical contact to be effective? Does telekinesis alter the work of muscles? Or does something else entirely different happen in the "Hepp" experiments?

In order to be able to describe telekinesis more exactly and to be able to use it more effectively, experiments and further exact observations and comparative considerations are still needed.

4. Telekinesis or Steering of Chance?

The already described extensive exclusion of coincidence in the dice games with my two children can first of all be explained in two basic ways: First, telekinesis could be at work, and second, chance could be guided.

In the telekinesis model, a non-physical force acts on the movements of the cube, in the random steering model, one influences chance. The telekinesis with its force model stands closer to the physical world description, while the chance model stands closer to the magic world descriptions, in which among other things with rituals the "meaningful coincidences" are directed.

When rolling the dice there is not much time for magical influence, so it is effective to know some time in advance which number is needed and to roll the dice before the other players can concentrate on a telekinetic disturbing action ... But this fact says only something about the circumstances in which this form of telekinesis or chance steering is practiced, but not about what actually happens.

With the other "Hepp" experiments like e.g. the karate punches the explanation model of the chance steering becomes rather bulky up to useless – there the telekinesis model is clearly more elegant.

Thus, it can be said first of all that in general the telekinesis model describes the previous experimental results better than the chance steering model.

So far, there are two indications that telekinesis behaves similar to a physical force from the point of view of its effect (i.e. on the receiver side): In the paper wheel experiment, the speed of rotation is halved when the mass of the paper wheel is doubled, and in the Levitation experiments (person on a chair), the telekinetic force of four people is more efectiv than the force of three people.

Now, in the paper wheel experiments, there was the phenomenon that the telekinesis on the transmitter side does not behave like a physical force: Four people together do not turn a paper wheel faster than a single person. Is there something similar in the "Hepp" experiments?

First of all, there are the following phenomena:

- In the "Hepp" experiments is done in a group, the telekinesis of the individuals seems to stabilize.
- Physical strength plus telekinesis goes well beyond normal physical strength.
- There seems to be the attainment of a certain mood, which is a one-pointedness that can be achieved by laughter, a fit of laughter, or even by an emergency, and which increases the strength of a person's physical power by telekinesis to the level just needed.

An effect corresponding to the phenomenon of the constant rotation speed independent of the number of people involved and performing telekinesis is not discernible
for the time being.

5. Telekinesis and Telepathy

Telepathy and telekinesis are first of all quite similar: In telepathy an information is transmitted in a non-physical way and in telekinesis an effect is transmitted in a non-physical way.

One can also say that telepathy is the magical cognitive ability and telekinesis is the magical ability to act. This is, of course, a distinction based on the structure of the physical body – roughly speaking, the distinction between eyes, ears and nose for cognition and bones, muscles and tendons for action. Of course, the question arises whether this distinction makes sense in magic and is an accurate description.

5. a) Comparison

First of all, it can be said that there are indeed people who have a very fine telepathic perception, but who refuse to act magically. The opposite case, on the other hand, is rather rare – i.e. acting magically but not perceiving anything. So telepathy and telekinesis do not have to occur at the same time or, more precisely, they do not both have to be used by one person in the same measure.

For a greater relationship between telepathy and telekinesis speaks first of all that they are both non-physical connections. They also both feel quite similar.

However, this telepathy/telekinesis feeling is not so easy to describe – it is a kind of "silent warmth", a kind of heightened awareness, and a more or less conscious expansion of consciousness.

I don't know, though, if this is just my way of perceiving it, or if it's general, since it's not exactly easy to talk to others about this subject in a sufficiently precise way …

There are also cases where it is difficult or impossible to distinguish whether telepathy or telekinesis is present. For example, my grandfather, in order to save his wife, needed quite a lot of money and therefore played the lottery and also very soon had six right numbers. Did he now telepathically foreknow the numbers or did he telekinetically influence the drawing of numbers?

Presumably the telekinesis is the more energy-consuming method, but one cannot exclude it – particularly since my grandfather, when he went once because of his knees to a healer, all the feathers of the chicken, which the healer was just plucking, flew towards him … whereupon the healer said to my grandfather that she could do nothing for him, for he has considerably greater forces than she had.

Foreknowledge (telepathy) and magic influence (telekinesis) cannot be distinguished always surely.

Albert Einstein has concluded from the indistinguishability of the centrifugal force and the gravitation in some experiments that both must be the same force – from which then finally the relativity theory has resulted. However, it is questionable whether the indistinguishability of telepathy and telekinesis in some cases can also be the starting point for such far-reaching conclusions and findings – but one can try …

There are even more cases where telepathy and telekinesis cannot be clearly distinguished.

There is the possibility to shift with one's own consciousness into the body of another person and not only communicate with the organs and chakras there, but also to treat them – e.g. by healing the hara (the chakra just below the navel) a much greater stability of the person concerned can be established. On the one hand this is telepathy, because one perceives something that is not directly accessible to the physical sense organs, and on the other hand it is telekinesis, because one changes something in the condition of the other person. However, this distinction is of little importance for one's own experience of what one does during such a chakra treatment. It is in the end just "contact to the chakra".

A very similar case is the treatment of a panic attack, in which one also crosses with one's own consciousness over into the body of the other person and partially redirects the life force, which accumulates in the three upper chakras during the panic, into the three lower chakras.

Another case is remote hypnosis, in which one hypnotizes a person who is several miles away and instructs him to do something specific. Telepathy is obvious in this case, because one is sending information to someone else in a non-physical way, but is the term 'telepathy' sufficient for interfering with the will of the other person and persuading him to do a certain action? For this, one must clearly expand the term 'telepathy' at least in comparison to its usual meaning.

One can approach this demarcation attempt between telepathy and telekinesis also from another side: In the physical sense there is in perception a definite direction – from the object to the perceiver.

However, this is not the case with telepathy: one can both receive and send out thoughts and images – "seeing" and "hearing" are, so to speak, indentical in telepathy. Sending out thoughts and images as in chakra healing, panic calming, remote hypnosis or simply summoning another person is therefore actually a telekinetic process, because one causes an effect.

5. b)   Expansion of Consciousness

It looks, therefore, as if telepathy and telekinesis are two aspects of the same 'magical activity'. This 'magical activity' can best be described as an expansion of one's own consciousness.

This working hypothesis has a great advantage in that it describes both telepathy and telekinesis in an elegant way:

> The conscious mind is normally capable of perceiving its own body and moving it. From the point of view of the consciousness, one does nothing fundamentally different in telepathy and in telekinesis: One directs one's attention to something and concentrates one's will on this something – this can be a precise perception but also an action.
>
> If one understands telepathy and telekinesis as an extension of one's own consciousness, the paper wheel becomes a part of one's own body – which means that one turns oneself, i.e. the paper wheel as a part of one's own body. This may sound a little absurd at first, but it is still worthwhile to think through this model.
>
> Every form of telepathy can be easily explained or at least elegantly described, if the perceived becomes a part of one's own body, i.e. an object within one's own consciousness, simply by the expansion of one's own consciousness.
>
> In the same way the "Hepp" experiments can be described: For example, if one extends one's consciousness to the person lying on one's heels and calves, this person temporarily becomes a part of one's own body, which one can then move effortlessly.
>
> Hypnosis and remote hypnosis are also an "extension of one's own consciousness to another person", which the hypnotizer also experiences very clearly in this way: during hypnosis, the hypnotist displaces the waking consciousness of the hypnotized from the body of the hypnotized, which also feels very invasive and conquering to the hypnotist. One of the first effects that occurs is that the hypnotized person can no longer move – the hypnotist has extended his consciousness to the hypnotized person's body and can therefore now determine the hypnotized person's movements.
>
> This phenomenon is also found in another place: If one wants to learn astral projection, a common way is to first relax, become quite still and motionless, then heavy and then warm, until finally one begins to vibrate and then after a while detaches from the physical body and then leaves it and floats above one's own physical body.
>
> The relaxation, the heaviness and the motionlessness mean that one lets go

of one's own physical body – after all, one wants to leave one's own body and for that one has to give up control over it. So one does with oneself exactly what the hypnotist does with the hypnotized during hypnosis: one detaches the consciousness from the body, one displaces it from the body – the focus is shifted from the waking consciousness to the subconsciousness.

With the working hypothesis of the expansion of consciousness one can describe different magical actions like telepathy, telekinesis, hypnosis and astral projection - whereby the phenomena coinciding with these processes become clear only by this description. Most striking is the control over one's own body and over the bodies of others or over objects.

This working hypothesis naturally entails some changes in the ideas about consciousness and about the relation between consciousness and body. One could almost say that magic is control over one's own body and over the surrounding space – which explains not least the intense charisma of most more advanced magicians …

6. Sword and Shield

If the occupation of space by one's own consciousness and especially the extension of one's own consciousness to other people and things is so essential in telepathy and telekinesis, then it makes sense and is even necessary to take care of one's own surrounding space.

In connection with my consultations I have repeatedly found that many people have no feeling for their surrounding space. Such people are mostly ascetics, victims and fans, i.e. they do without, withdraw, make themselves small, are rather defenseless, give far too much, receive little, are exploited, tend to burnout, are unable to separate themselves from other persons, etc.

Therefore, over the years, I have come up with a few "games" that can help you become aware of your surroundings.

There are two distances that are important in these games. The "individual surronding area" or the "aura" extends approximately to the wrist of the outstretched arm, give or take 60cm.

The first boundary is where the auras of two persons touch, that is, at the distance at which the two people could place their palms against each other with their arms outstretched – that is, at a distance of about 120cm.

The second boundary is where one could touch the body of the other with his flat hand – i.e. at a distance of 60cm.

Reaching these two distances feels quite different: at 120cm it is a reletively peaceful first touch of the other, at 60cm it is a rather aggressive intrusion into the other's area.

6. a) Game 1

One person stands in the room with eyes closed and a second person walks slowly and quietly towards the first person. When the first person feels that the other person is coming into their space, they say "now" or something similar. Then the second person stands still and both compare their perceptions.

The second person approaches the first person in turn once from the front, once from behind, once from the right and once from the left. Most of the time the distances at which the first person says that the other is coming into her space differ very clearly. Sometimes the first person does not perceive anything at all on one of the four sides.

6. b) Game 2

One person stands in the room with eyes open and a second person walks slowly toward the first person. When the first person feels that the other person is coming into their space, they say "Stop."

If the second person finds this "stop" convincing, he stops – if not, he continues walking …

In this game, the first person may feel intense emotions, remember previous situations of boundary violation, etc.

6. c) Game 3

The first person stands in the room with eyes open and looks for an "ally": his own soul, Christ, an oak tree, a tiger … whatever feels suitable for the person as an "ally". The first person then imagines this ally at a appropriate place close by.

Then the second person walks toward the first, and the first says "stop" again when it senses the second person entering its space.

The first person keeps looking for "allies" until he found one with whom saying "stop" has enough force to stop the second person.

Then you look to see if the distance at which the first person says "stop" is actually comfortable for the first person. If it is not, continue the game until the first person can make the second person stop by saying "Stop" at a distance that is comfortable for the first person.

6. d) Game 4

Now the same arrangement as in the previous game is used, but the first person does not say anything, but tries to stop the second person without words at a distance comfortable to the first person just by imagining to say "Stop!" or the like.

6. e)   Game 5

The starting position is again the same, but the first person not only says "Stop!" inwardly, but imagines that the second person will, for example, turn around, pass the first person on the left, or something similar.

6. f)   Game 6

The five previous games have dealt with the left "shield arm", i.e. with the defense, but in a rather slow, deliberate way. From this game on, faster defense variations are coming.

Instead of walking towards the first person, the second person now forms an (imaginary) ball of light in his hand and then suddenly throws it at the first person. The first person watches to see if he can notice where this ball of light hits him. When the first person has recognized the hit part of the body, the second person says where he threw the ball of light, so that the first person can see whether he has had a clear perception of this "life force attack" (and whether the second person can throw such life force balls with sufficient intensity …).

In this game the second person should not use his own life force, but get life force e.g. from the sun or from the earth.

6. g)   Game 7

The second person again throws light balls at the first person, who now deflects these light balls with an imagined shield or similar.

After each throw, the two people compare their impressions of whether the first person did a good job of deflecting the light ball.

6. h)   Game 8

Now the roles are reversed: the first person goes towards the second person and tries to enter their aura and the second person fends off the first person – this is now an attack with the right "sword arm".

6. i) Game 9

Now the light-ball game is played with reversed roles: the first person throws life-force balls at the second person.

After each throw, both compare again their impression of how well the light ball was thrown and where it may have hit or should have hit.

6. j) Game 10

Now they look together to see where the first person's weak points are or where there is still potential for improvement, whereupon the two then think up a game with the help of which this weak point can be healed or this potential can be realized.

6. k) Consideration of the results

These games are used to get a feeling for the life force and especially for one's own surrounding space ("aura"). This can have a great practical benefit and help, for example, to avoid being exploited, to avert a threatening burnout, to better assert oneself, etc.

These games show another aspect of telekinesis than the paper wheel experiment and the "Hepp" experiments: In these games one perceives one's surroundings and what happens in it and near it – and ideally learns to protect and preserve one's own space.

> - In the paper wheel experiments, telekinesis acts "by life force" directly on an object.

> - In the "Hepp" experiments, telekinesis "by life force" amplifies the force in the muscles many times over.

> - In the games, one perceives and reacts to the physically approaching life force (aura) of the other or the telekinetically thrown life force balls of the other.

These three types of experiments can be summarized in an overview in two ways.

The first of these two overviews shows what affects what, i.e. in what framework telekinesis takes place:

Types of telekinetic influence I	
Experiment	*Effect*
Paper wheel experiment	life force => object
Hepp experiment	life force/muscles => object
Games	life force => life force

The second overview shows basically the same sorting, only this time systematically sorted by sender and receiver:

Types of telekinetic influence II			
		Receiver	
		physisch	*life force*
	physical	normal action	
Sender	*physical and life force*	Hepp experiment	
	life force	paper wheel experiment	games

Since there are two free spaces in this overview, the question arises if there could be actions that would fit into these two places.

A physical action that acts on the life force would be, for example, breathing exercises such as pranayama or kundalini meditations, which both increase the life force in the body and move it.

A physical action that is amplified by the life force and acts on the life force would be, for example, ritual actions with words and gestures that are intended to heal a chakra, for example.

By these two examples the overview can be completed:

Types of telekinetic influence III			
		Receiver	
		physisch	*life force*
Sender	*physical*	normal action	breathing exercises
	physical and life force	Hepp experiment	rituals
	life force	paper wheel experiment	games

Now you can add also another column "physical and life force" to the recipients in this overview and see if there are processes that correspond to the three new fields created by this.

For the effect of "physical and life force" on "physical and life force" one does not need to search long: that is life as a whole ... All processes where not both are involved are special cases. One could also quote a karate-fight as a more dramatic example of this kind of interaction.

When do physical things affect "physical and life force"? Probably physical things always affect both – a case where this is particularly clear is e.g. the emergence of a trauma, because thereby both the psyche is fundamentally changed and the part of the life force corresponding to this part of the psyche is encapsulated.

When does the life force act on "physical and life force"? For this purpose, e.g. homeopathy comes into question – in the globules only the information of the original substance is contained, i.e. the information imprinted into the life force, but not the original substance itself.

Types of telekinetic influence IV			
		Receiver		
		physisch	*physical and life force*	*life force*
	physical	normal action	trauma emergence	breathing exercises
Sender	physical and life force	Hepp experiment	life (karate-fight)	rituals
	life force	paper wheel experiment	homeopathy	games

In order to prove telekinesis in principle, an experiment is needed in which only the life force acts on a physical object – otherwise it cannot be proved with certainty: the paper wheel experiment.

However, once telekinesis is proven in principle, one can also consider all new possible forms of effects – which puts telekinesis into a larger context and even includes procedures like homeopathy.

The effect of the homeopathic glubules can also be described with the working hypothesis of the expansion of consciousness: By taking the globules, one allows the original substance (animal, plant, mineral) from which this pellet has been made to influence one's own condition. As a result, the consciousness of the animal, plant or stone in question expands to the person who has taken this remedy and changes the person in a way that corresponds to the character of the animal, plant or stone.

The same is true of trauma: When it occurs, a part of the psyche and therefore of the life force body is isolated from the rest of the psyche and life force body. This area is therefore largely withdrawn from the consciousness and thus from the control by the consciousness until it is healed, i.e. until it is reintegrated into the psyche and the life force body.

Telepathy, telekinesis and in general magic are therefore also a question of what the consciousness has access to and of what not.

7. Telekinesis and Analogies

In magic many analogies are used. There are also "analogy-effects" independent of the magician like astrology.

Analogies dependent on a magician are, for example, homeopathy, where the substance from which the globules taken by the sick person are made must correspond as exactly as possible to the patient's illness.

Therefore, one can at least once ask the question whether there is a connection between telekinesis and analogies.

In the telekinesis experiments considered so far, the analogies did not play any recognizable role – if one leaves aside homeopathy. In homeopathy the analogies are important, but the telekinesis is limited to the fact that the essence of the substance, from which the globules have been made, presumably extends its consciousness to the psyche and the body of the sick person and thereby heals him.

8. Apollo and Dionysus

The distinction between Apollonian and Dionysian is probably not too important in understanding telepathy and telekinesis, but it does make a difference both in the practice of telepathy and telekinesis and in their application.

Apollo is the god of the sun and of rightness – just as almost all the sun gods from Baldur to Dagda to Ra are the maintainers of rightness.

Apollo, like Baldur, is more a god of rightness than a sun god – the role of the sun god is much clearer among the Greeks in Helios.

People with an Apollonian attitude are looking for the natural order in the world, for the holy state within themselves, for the universal harmony … for Ma'ath, Fhrinne, Me, Tashi, Ho'zhong and whatever else this rightness has been called in the different ancient languages. The goal is a glow, a radiance from the heart chakra, the experience of oneself as an integrated part of the whole.

People with a Dionysian attitude look for intensity in life, for dance, for sexual union, for intoxication, for dissolution of boundaries, for novelty … for the exciting, for the thrilling. The goal is the life fire of Kundalini, the experience of uninhibited self-expression.

The Apollonian has as method the contemplation, the concentration, the imagination, the ordering, the insertion, the organic growth, the cooperation, the non-contradiction in the motivation and in the implementation …

The Dionysian has as method the laughter, the fun, the ecstasy, the sexuality, the violent feelings, the increase, the contradiction, the fight, the overcoming, the intoxication, the egocentricity in the motivation and in the realization …

Now these two descriptions are certainly neither complete nor completely free from subjective distortions by me, but perhaps they show that also telepathy and telekinesis can be stimulated and created in at least two fundamentaly different ways.

9. Telekinesis for Advanced Learners

In the case of telepathy, the experiences and findings could be well divided into two books: "Telepathy for Beginners" and "Telepathy for Advanced Learners".

With telekinesis, however, I have so little experience with "advanced telekinesis" that it is only enough for one chapter "Telekinesis for Advanced Learners" and not for a whole book.

9. a) A flying candle

The clearest case of advanced telekinesis I experienced at the beginning of my time as a "sorcerer's apprentice", when my magic teacher Axel conjured a demon together with me in his room. Thereby a candle, which was standing on a holder on the wall, received a violent blow as if from an invisible person, by which the candle flew through the room and then rolled into a corner.

9. b) Lifting heavy loads

The example already given of the mother lifting a truck in order to be able to rescue her child who is trapped under the wheel is also a clear case of advanced telekinesis.

9. c) Remote Shocks

Another example is "remote shocks" that Frater U.D. told me about and that he himself has experienced and can perform. Since I have known him for a long time, I believe him that such a thing is possible – and one can also feel whether someone can do such a thing, which I have no doubt about in his case.

In such a "long-distance thrust" a person makes a thrusting gesture in the direction of another person several meters away, who thereby receives a thrust without any physical contact and possibly falls over. This method is also possible without a gesture.

Such techniques are found in Far Eastern martial arts and elite military units.

9. d)   Hypnosis

When extending one's own consciousness to other people, whereby one can direct these people, it is unclear whether this should be counted among advanced telepathy or among advanced telekinesis.

As I have quite a lot of experience with hypnosis myself, it seems to me that this is a kind of "advanced telepythy/telekinesis", where one takes more or less complete control over the body of the other person with one's own consciousness.

By "complete control" is meant that one can, for example, make another person temporarily think he is a dog and run on all fours and bite some other person.

9. e)   "Analogy telekinesis"

There is a form of telekinesis that also uses an analogy. This experiment is attributed to Aleister Crowley – whether this attribution is correct is, as with such things, always doubtful. However, the experiment itself sounds plausible.

A person walks behind another walking person and imitates as closely as possible their way of walking. This creates an analogy bond between the two people. Because of this binding, the second (rear) person can cause the first person to stumble by a sudden movement of his own, so that the first person falls down.

I have experienced such a case of analogy telekinesis myself – so I know that this is possible to do.

This experiment can be attributed to the "steering of people", whereby usually more gestures are used than e.g. in remote hypnosis.

9. f)   Preotecting the surrounding space

The extension and generalization of this "steering of people" is the control of one's own extended surrounding space – i.e. not only the independence within the radius of half a meter as in the ten described "games", but within a radius of ten meters.

It is quite a violent experience to sit next to a person who has this extended surrounding space control – it is hard to maintain one's own space and keep one's own course within his range.

Rudiments of this ability of " surrounding space control" are found in people who "fill" a space as soon as they enter it – without having to do anything. These people tend to be dominant, i.e. they mostly belong to the addict/perpetrator/star-extreme –

but possibly the "space-control" is not necessarily bound to this extreme.

9. g) Leviation

Another kind of telekinesis are levitations, i.e. levitating objects or oneself, which I have not yet experienced myself, but which is reported from cultures as different as the Indian yogis and the Christian saints. This does not prove this phenomenon, but it makes it at least so probable that one should consider it.

The already mentioned lifting of people only with the index fingers is no levitation in the narrower sense, but at least it is quite similar to levitation.

9. h) Materializations

Should one also count materializations to telekinesis? Telekinesis is strictly speaking the moving of objects without physical contact. With materializations, however, an object appears (or disappears) completely. In the end it doesn't matter if you count materializations to telekinesis or not, because both are related processes – the experience of a materialization makes the possibility of advanced telekinesis much more probable.

> My own most impressive experience with a materialization happend some years ago. At that time I had a major crisis and wondered what to do next. Finally I came to the conclusion that I really have to let go of everything completely, so that what I actually am can show itself. At that time I was visiting a friend in Offenburg.
>
> At this decision I was standing at a traffic island in the middle of a crossroads, where this traffic island was set up as a crosswalk – you could walk into the middle from all sides and from there to where you wanted to go. This small circular place in the middle of the traffic circle is surrounded by about eight upright stones about the height of a man – a "mini-stonehenge".
>
> So I went to one of these stones and squatted down in front of it and took off the gold Christ necklace and the silver dragon necklace, both of which I wore at these days all the time, and put them on the ground in front of the stone and said, "For the one for whom they are intended." Then I looked at them for a moment and left.
>
> About three months later I was traveling from Freiburg to Bonn and had a

one and a half hour stop at the Offenburg train station. Something drew me to the stone circle on the traffic island and although I told myself that it was silly and sentimental to think of my two necklaces, I followed the impulse and went there. When I got there, I squatted down in front of the stone where I had laid down my two chains. Of course, they were not there anymore – gold and silver do not stay long in a busy public place …

I was a little sad that I no longer had the two chains. When I wanted to get up and go away, I looked again at the foot of the stone – and suddenly my two chains were there again. I can hardly describe how that felt. That was actually not possible – that was really magic or something even greater.

Either the two chains had just materialized again (and "dematerialized" before) or the two chains had been invisible for three months. Materialization seems more likely to me, since the place was very clean and had obviously been swept regularly and all weeds and the like removed.

9. i) Results

One may wonder whether the distinction between simple and advanced telekinesis is at all meaningful.

The difference that seems to me to argue for separating these two forms is the contrast between paper-wheel telekinesis, which can be performed at any time and by almost anyone, but is very weak, and such actions as lifting a truck in an emergency, which occur spontaneously, but where the telekinesis is very strong.

The different variants of the Hepp attempt seem to me to belong to simple, ordinary telekinesis, since they can also be performed by almost anyone at any time.

On the other hand, the long-distance blows in martial arts or the blows (from an "invisible person or ghost") against candles in demon evocations are advanced, extraordinary telekinesis with a great effect, which, however, occurs spontaneously.

However, it is also possible to learn advanced telekinesis with a not perfect, but reasonably regular reliability. The basis for this is – as far as I can see – learning to control one's own extended surrounding space including people, animals, plants and other things in this surrounding space. This "martial form of magic", if you want to call it that, is however something I have so far avoided and with which I have hardly any experience – I am currently still examining whether and if so, in what form I actually want to learn it.

The extraordinary telekinesis, however, does not have to be warlike as e.g. the reports about the Aboriginals in Australia show, who can heal the broken bone of one of their tribe members by a common ritual by telekinesis. I have never been present at such a healing, but a friend of mine, who had a very badly bent spine, was treated by the Cypriot healer Daskalos, who died some years ago, by "laying on of hands", after which she had a perfectly straight spine and could become a dancer – the X-ray pictures of her spine before and after the healing did not have much similarity with each other ...

Such a healing is also an invasive process, i.e. a massive intervention from the outside, but it does not serve to assert oneself against others, but to heal another person. Of course, the two are not mutually exclusive, but the extension of one's possibilities to such forms of telekinesis naturally requires a review of one's principles.

These standards for one's own behavior will be different for each person, as in all areas of life – and these standards of a cerrain person will be the same in all these advanced forms of magic as well as in the rest of the life of this person. But a little awareness in dealing with this "extraordinary telekinesis" cannot hurt.

10. Telekinesis Models

For an area that is so little researched, it is difficult to come up with a model – at best a working hypothesis is possible.

10. a) Life force

The simplest and so far the only known model is the life force, which is emitted and thus moves the life force of an object and thus the object itself. This model has the advantage that it forms a good basis to be able to imagine a helpful image when practicing telekinesis: e.g. a ray of light coming from the hand and pushing and turning the paper wheel.

This model has the further advantage that with the term "life force" one can also describe such sensations as the pressure in the palms of the hands during life force healings or when absorbing sunlight, the spinning in the chakras, the heat of Kundalini and the like.

So the concept and the term of life force helps at least to describe different magical phenomena like telekinesis and telepathy in a uniform way.

Another advantage is that in many old languages and cultures have a term for this life force like e.g. the Egyptian "Ankh", the Indian "Prana" and the "Holy Spirit" of Christianity. The concept of the life force therefore enables the connection to several ancient world views.

Also in some healing methods the life force is a central element – e.g. in Reiki and in homeopathy. Likewise, the basic magical-spiritual experience of astral projection can be described with the help of the life force as the temporary separation of a person's life force body from his physical body.

However, if one wants to define more precisely what life force is and how it behaves, it gets more difficult. However, one can describe some characteristics of the life force:

- It is a kind of non-physical "force-substance," that is, it can be moved like a substance and it can exert an effect like a force.

- It can be felt as heat and perceived as a milky white glow with a slight blue glow.

- The life force can contain information, i.e. it can be imprinted – e.g. when sending a telepathic message.

- It can organize itself and become a life force body belonging to a human being, an animal, a plant, a stone, a lake, a star, a deity, etc.. This self-organisation of the life force results in the formation of the chakras.

This aspect of the life force ultimately results in a pantheistic view of the world, i.e. in the idea of a total animate world containing both life and consciousness in every smallest element.

- The whole psyche is a content of the life force body. "Psyche" and "life-force body" are thus largely the same thing, except that the psyche is not normally thought to be able to leave the body – apart from the process described in psychology as "dissociation".

The life force is thus substance, psyche, spirits/gods and information.

The fact that the life force can only be described, but not explained, is no argument against it, because every science consists only of observations, which are described afterwards. Thereby it is striven to find regularities in different phenomena and to describe these then in as simple and comprehensive a way as possible – until one has found the "world formula" in the end.

Science is thus nothing else than the systematic, as uniform as possible and contradiction-free description of observations.

Something else is not possible also in the magic: One accomplishes experiments, observes the phenomena arising thereby, looks for regularities, describes these regularities, draws conclusions from the regularities and examines these conclusions with the help of new experiments.

In the ideal case the described regularities, which altogether form the "model", result in one or the other practical application possibility – in physics e.g. the building of an airplane and in magic e.g. a healing possibility.

10. b) Yesod and Da'ath

As in many areas of magic, there seem to be two areas of telekinesis: an easy and almost anytime producible form, which is quite weak, and a much more difficult producible form, which is much stronger, but which cannot be executed so easily reliably and at any time.

One can describe these two forms of magic with the help of two terms from the Kabbalah: Yesod (ordinary magic) and Da'ath (extraordinary magic). In the first case, only the life force of one's own life force body (Yesod) works; in the second case, the life force of a deity (Da'ath) also works.

The difference between these two forms of magic is partly described in fantasy literature as for example in the "Quest of the Riddle-Master" trilogy by Patricia McKillip or in the "Kingslayer" trilogy by Patrick Rothfuss.

In order to be able to exercise "extraordinary telekinesis" systematically and not only spontaneously out of an emergency situation or the like, one needs access to Da'ath, i.e. to the boundaryless realm in which the deities are – which means among other things that one must be able to give up one's own boundary to the world. It may sound very abstract, but this process is very concrete and intense. It is described by almost all mystics on their "journey to God".

This "boundaryless state" is also described by Buddha, among others, as the four boundaryless qualities: boundless equanimity (composure), boundaryless compassion (perceiving everything), boundaryless love (experiencing everything as unity) and boundaryless joy (being in harmony with everything).

This dissolution of boundaries is, among other things, also the expansion of one's own consciousness and one's own ability to act in the surrounding space – the "miracles".

The step into this boundary-less state is always at the same place on this path – no matter which system one uses and how strongly this path has been differentiated: It is on the path from here to now to the oneness (God, Nirvana) the fourth of five, thus the fourth part, if one breaks this path down into five equal parts.

> 1. The starting point is one's own body in the world in the here and now – one looks at things from the outside. Here one is outside-oriented (Kabbalah: Malkuth).

> 2. By meditation, prayers, dream journeys, rituals, magic etc. the world of life force is discovered – one looks at things from the inside and sees them as mostly a slightly blurred and only little colored vision in a room filled with a diffuse light. Here one is life-force oriented (Kabbalah: Yesod).

> 3. Behind the area of life-force one finds one's own soul – which shines intensely and colorfully from within. Here one rests in oneself and radiates from one's own center (Kabbalah: Tiphareth).

> 4. When "resting in oneself" one does not need any delimitation outwardly anymore and can experience oneself as part of an all-encompassing continuum – here the deities appear as shining contours in the light. One becomes a part of the "sea of divinity", of which one's own soul is a "drop" (Kabbalah: Da'ath).

> 5. Finally, one reaches the underlying unity, God, the glistening white light (Kabbalah: Kether).

This is only a very brief description of this path, which should give a little orientation, what is meant by the area, from which the extraordinary magic and also the extraordinary telekinesis can be exercised, from which thus "miracles" can be accomplished.

In India this way is described by the yoga. The ability to perform miracles ("Siddhis"), which occurs thereby, is regarded in India rather skeptically and above all as a distraction from the essential.

In Tibet this path is called "Lamrim". In contrast to India, in Tibet the occurrence of miracles is downright expected and regarded as a proof of the inner progress.

In Judaism, the miracles of the prophets have been understood as gifts of God.

Christianity has a very similar view and vehemently argues (contrary to the statements of Christ himself) that humans cannot perform the same miracles as Christ.

Among the Sufis in Islam, the miracles are also well known, but there is a tradition not to speak about these miracles in order not to attract disturbing attention.

In magic, the miracles, that is, the "extraordinary magic" itself is the goal – the development towards the state of detachment is here only a means to an end, which, however, may well fundamentally change the magician who reaches this state.

10. c) Expansion of Consciousness

The second model completely dispenses with the concept of life force and describes telekinesis and also all other forms of magic with the help of the expansion of consciousness into the surrounding space as well as the things, plants, animals and people in this surrounding space.

This model is much simpler, since it is based only on the assumption that the consciousness can perceive and direct everything to which it extends – as if these things were "conquered" by one's own consciousness and thus would become a part of one's own body.

In this magic model there is also hardly a technique, because one does simply ehat one does – there is no difference to moving one's own hand.

Of course, one can ask how from this model the observed difference between ordinary magic and extraordinary magic can be explained – probably simply by the quality of the consciousness expansion:

> - In ordinary magic in Yesod, one expands one's consciousness only a little, i.e., one stretches one's perception and ability to act a little toward something outside oneself.

- In the extraordinary magic in Da'ath, one completely dissolves one's boundaries to the outside and can therefore extend one's own consciousness to something else at will and then influence this to a great extent.

How can one explain the "telekinesis constant" from this model? It still remains a mystery for the time being …

One could assume that in ordinary telekinesis (Yesod) only a certain "part" of consciousness, a certain "amount" of consciousness or a similarly limited amount of influence can reach another object or thing – but in the end this is also only a description of what is observed and does not relate this observation to any other phenomenon.

10. d)   Extension of Consciousness and Life Force

If one conceives of the life force as the perception of one consciousness by another consciousness, vital force becomes an element in the "consciousness-extension" model. Then the life force is no longer a "non-physical sub-stance", but just an image in one's own consciousness, which arises when one perceives something directly from consciousness to consciousness, i.e. telepathically. This would explain, among other things, why gestures can be helpful in telekinesis – they facilitate the extension of the consciousness to something that is outside of one's own body.

With this perception is not meant the perception of the consciousness as in meditation, thus the direct self-perception "from the inside", but the perception of the consciousness "from the outside" in another person or object.

This interpretation of the life force can probably be made more easily understandable with the help of an overview. First of all, there are five directions in which an effect can take place:

- from the body to the body: physics
- from the body to one's own consciousness: perception
- from the consciousness to one's own body: impulse to act
- from consciousness to one's own consciousness: self-awareness
- from consciousness to another consciousness: telepathy, telekinesis

When the consciousness perceives itself directly, this is simply self-awareness: I am aware that I am aware of myself. For this, no detour, no aid or the like is necessary.

However, if one perceives another consciousness, this consciousness is not directly connected with one's own consciousness, i.e. a process of perception must take place.

A process of perception, however, creates an "image": the image when seeing, the sound when hearing, the scent when smelling, etc. The telepathic perception of another consciousness should therefore also create such a picture – and the "substance" of this "picture" is the life force.

Presumably this is an optical perception, because the consciousness of humans is filled above all by optical impressions, since the seeing is by far the most important sense perception of humans. The life force has probably simply "borrowed" the milky white glow from the optical memories in the brain – and supplements it from time to time with heat sensations, as for example with Kundalini.

From this results in the reverse conclusion that the ability to willfully imagine symbols and the like, i.e. to imagine them vividly optically, can direct the life force – whereby life force is here again the perception of the consciousness. This willful imagination is the core of magic: By the inner image one attains the contact with the life force, i.e. with the consciousness side of the things on which this imagination is directed. By these images one expands one's own consciousness to the consciousness of another person, an object or a whole situation.

According to this model, the life force is the optical representation of the perceptions between one's own consciousness and another consciousness.

- - -

A more detailed description of the connections between physics and the life force as well as a more detailed model of magic can be found in my book "The Synthesis of Physics and Magic".

11. Learning Telekinesis

To give a general instruction to learn something is not possible in the end, because people are too different – "every Jeck is different", as they say here in the Rhineland (a "Jeck" is a costumed participant of carnival).

But it is at least possible to sketch a map of the area in which one moves – although there is by no means always agreement between all those who deal with the subject. So the following is in the end above all just "my map".

To learn telekinesis there is nothing better than to experiment with telekinesis – without practical experience no familiarity with a subject and no expertise in this field can develop.

So it makes sense to perform the experiments described in this book yourself: the spinning of the paper wheel, the "surrounding space games" and the different variants of the "Hepp" experiment.

Since telekinesis and telepathy are closely related, all telepathy exercises and telepathy games are also helpful to get to know telekinesis better. Hypnosis also belongs to these telepathy/telekinesis phenomena.

These "psi-phenomena" are closely connected with the life force or at least can be described with the help of the life force. Therefore, all activities that have to do with the life force and are therefore suitable to get a more conscious contact with the life force are helpful for learning telekinesis: breathing exercises (pranayama), life force guidance (Reiki etc.), feeling or seeing acupuncture points and meridians, dream journeys, consecrations, drawing protective circles, invocations … so ultimately almost all areas of magic.

According to one's own disposition and inclinations, one will probably soon develop a focus: healings, consecrations, hypnosis, battle magic, talisman magic, invocations, evocations … The area that suits you the most will probably also be the area in which you will achieve success the fastest.

In general, in everything one does, a clear motivation is conducive: knowledge, power, curiosity, spirit of research, desire to heal … This also applies to one's own occupation with telekinesis.

There is another element, which is helpful for almost all undertakings: At the beginning of your research you can ask for help from "above" – from your own soul, from a deity – whatever. This has the advantage that suitable opportunities, know-ledgeable people, informative books and the like will be sent to you …

English Books by Harry Eilenstein

- Living Magic (261 p.)
- The Synthesis of Physics and Magic (192 p.)
- Telepathy for Beginners (60 p.)
- Telekinesis for Beginners (56 p.)
- Astral Projection for Beginners (60 p.)
- Invocations for Beginners (52 p.)
- Evocations for Beginners (62 p.)
- Auto-Movement for Beginners (60 p.)
- Elves for Beginners (56 p.)
- Hypnosis for Beginners (56 p.)
- Money Magic for Beginners (60 p.)
- Magic Objects for Beginners (64 p.)
- Shamanism for Beginners (52 p.)
- Crop Circles for Beginners (344 p.)
- Number Symbolism for Beginners (64 p.)

These books will be puplished soon:

- Telepathy for Advanced Learners
- Life Force for Beginners

- Meditation for Beginners
- Kundalini for Beginners
- Chakra-Magic for Beginners
- Astrology for Beginners
- Ritual Magic for Beginners
- Mandalas for Beginners
- Love Magic for Beginners
- Magic Research for Beginners
- Self-awareness for Beginners
- Symbolism of Numbers for Beginners
- Language of the Moon – for Beginners
- Magic Chant for Beginners
- Prophecy for Beginners
- Da'ath-Magic for Beginners
- Feng Shui for Beginners
- Magic for Beginners – Anthology I
- Magic for Beginners – Anthology II
- Magic for Beginners – Anthology III
- Magic for Beginners – Anthology IV

Bücher von Harry Eilenstein

Religion allgemein
- Die sieben Schritte des Lebens (428 S.)
- Muttergöttin und Schamanen (168 S.)
- Göbekli Tepe (472 S.)
- Die Göttin von Göbekli Tepe (144 S.)
- Totempfähle (440 S.)
- Christus (60 S.)
- Dakini (80 S.)
- Vajra (76 S.)

Ägypten
- Hathor und Re 1: Götter und Mythen im Alten Ägypten (432 S.)
- Hathor und Re 2: Die altägyptische Religion – Ursprünge, Kult und Magie (396 S.)
- Isis (508 S.)

Indogermanen
- Die Entwicklung der indogermanischen Religionen (700 S.)
- Wurzeln und Zweige der indogermanischen Religion (224 S.)

Germanen
- Die Götter der Germanen (87 Bände – siehe nächste Seite)
- Odin (300 S.)

Kelten
- Cernunnos (690 S.)
- Taliesin (228 S.)
- Der Kessel von Gundestrup (220 S.)
- Der Chiemsee-Kessel (76)

Psychologie
- Über die Freude (100 S.)
- Das Geheimnis des inneren Friedens (252 S.)
- Das Beziehungsmandala (52 S.)
- Gefühle und ihre Verwandlungen (404 S.)
- einsgerichtet (140 S.)
- Liebe und Eigenständigkeit (216 S.)
- Von innerer Fülle zu äußerem Gedeihen (52 S.)

Heilung
- Die Symbolik der Krankheiten (76 S.)

Kunst
- Herz des Tanzes – Tanz des Herzens (160 S.)

Drama
- König Athelstan (104 S.)

Bücher von Harry Eilenstein

„Magie für Anfänger"

- Telepathie für Anfänger (60 S.)
- Telepathie für Fortgeschrittene (52 S.)
- Telekinese für Anfänger (52 S.)
- Lebenskraft für Anfänger (60 S.)
- Meditation für Anfänger (56 S.)
- Kundalini für Anfänger (100 S.)
- Hypnose für Anfänger (56 S.)
- Auto-Movement für Anfänger (56 S.)
- Chakra-Magie für Anfänger (148 S.)
- Astralreisen für Anfänger (56 S.)
- Astrologie für Anfänger (120 S.)
- Ritual-Magie für Anfänger (56 S.)
- Mandalas für Anfänger (68 S.)
- Geldzauber für Anfänger (56 S.)
- Liebeszauber für Anfänger (52 S.)
- Invokationen für Anfänger (52 S.)
- Evokationen für Anfänger (60 S.)
- Elfen für Anfänger (56 S.)
- Magie-Forschung für Anfänger (140 S.)
- Selbsterkenntnis für Anfänger (52 S.)
- Zahlensymbolik für Anfänger (60 S.)
- Die Sprache des Mondes – für Anfänger (116 S.)
- Zaubergesänge für Anfänger (100 S.)
- Zukunftschau für Anfänger (60 S.)
- Schamanismus für Anfänger (52 S.)
- Magische Gegenstände für Anfänger (68 S.)
- Da'ath-Magie für Anfänger (64 S.)
- Kornkreise für Anfänger (348 S.)
- Feng Shui für Anfänger (96 S.)
- Magie für Anfänger – Sammelband I (696 S.)
- Magie für Anfänger – Sammelband II (664 S.)
- Magie für Anfänger – Sammelband III (580 S.)

„Traumreisen"

- Traumreisen zu Heilpflanzen (700 S.)

Magie

- Handbuch für Zauberlehrlinge (408 S.)
- Tarot (104 S.)
- Physik und Magie (184 S.)
- Die Synthese von Physik und Magie (200S.)
- Die Magie-Formel (156 S.)
- Krafttiere – Tiergöttinnen – Tiertänze (112 S.)
- Schwitzhütten (524 S.)
- Mythen und Magie der Harfe (116 S.)
- Magie heute – Berichte aus der Praxis (288 S.)

Meditation

- Der Lebenskraftkörper (230 S.)
- Die Chakren (100 S.)
- Das Chakren-System mit den Nebenchakren (296 S.)
- Organe und Chakren (64 S.)
- Die platonischen Körper in den Chakren (156 S.)
- Meditation (140 S.)
- Drachenfeuer (124 S.)
- Kundalini I (676 S.)
- Reinkarnation (156 S.)
- einsgerichtet (140 S.)

Astrologie

- Astrologie (496 S.)
- Photo-Astrologie (428 S.)
- Die astrologischen Aspekte (88 S.)
- Horoskop und Seele (120 S.)

Kabbala

- Kursus der praktischen Kabbala (150 S.)
- Eltern der Erde (450 S.)
- Blüten des Lebensbaumes:
    - Die Struktur des kabbalistischen Lebensbaumes (370 S.)
    - Der kabbalistische Lebensbaum als Forschungshilfsmittel (580 S.)
    - Der kabbalistische Lebensbaum als spirituelle Landkarte (520 S.)

Die Themen der 87 Bände der Reihe „Die Götter der Germanen"